The Secret Life of Rose

of related interest

The Ice-Cream Sundae Guide to Autism
An Interactive Kids' Book for Understanding Autism
By Debby Elley and Tori Houghton
Illustrated by J.C. Perry
ISBN 978 1 78775 380 8
eISBN 978 1 78775 381 5

Can't Not Won't
A Story About A Child Who Couldn't Go To School
By Eliza Fricker
ISBN 978 1 83997 520 2
eISBN 978 1 83997 521 9

The Red Beast
Helping Children on the Autism Spectrum
to Cope with Angry Feelings
By K.I. Al-Ghani
Illustrated by Haitham Al-Ghani
ISBN 978 1 83997 275 1
eISBN 978 1 83997 276 8

The Secret Life of Rose

Jodie Clarke and Rose Smitten

Foreword by Dr Luke Beardon

Illustrated by Rose Smitten

Jessica Kingsley Publishers
London and Philadelphia

First published in Great Britain in 2024 by Jessica Kingsley Publishers
An imprint of John Murray Press

1

The fonts, layout and overall design of this book have been prepared
according to dyslexia friendly principles. At JKP we aim to make
our books' content accessible to as many readers as possible.

A CIP catalogue record for this title is available from
the British Library and the Library of Congress

ISBN 978 1 80501 042 5
eISBN 978 1 80501 043 2

Printed and bound in China by Leo Paper Products

Jessica Kingsley Publishers' policy is to use papers that are natural,
renewable and recyclable products and made from wood grown in
sustainable forests. The logging and manufacturing processes are expected
to conform to the environmental regulations of the country of origin.

Jessica Kingsley Publishers
Carmelite House
50 Victoria Embankment
London EC4Y 0DZ

www.jkp.com

John Murray Press
Part of Hodder & Stoughton Ltd
An Hachette Company

Contents

Foreword

Dr Luke Beardon

Being in a position of privilege is such a privilege.
I am one of the luckiest people I am aware of in
that I get so many autistic insights from all sorts of
people from all walks of life. Each and every insight is
another layer of wonder for me, and just that bit more
of added illumination into the autistic lived experience.
And you — you lucky, privileged reader — now get to
read some of the amazing experiences from Rose and
Jodie, the wonderful duo who have opted to share
some words of reality 'through the autism lens' about
what it is really like to be autistic.

Rose gives us an astonishingly clear narrative on
a range of topics from stimming to meltdown to
masking to sensory issues to her unique skill set,
while Jodie offers her perspective on how Rose's
experiences might be understood in a broader sense.
Deeply personal, and definitely personable, this well-
written prose deserves a wide readership.

Both Rose and Jodie provide such honest opinions,
which go some way towards dispelling those pesky

autism myths; it was refreshing to say the least to
read about Rose's empathic abilities! It is impressive
how many gems of wisdom are packed into this
book; I found myself devouring it at speed – and
immediately returning to the beginning to allow myself
more time to digest what I was reading.

Thank you, Rose – for sharing your (not so) secret
life! I have no doubt whatsoever that in doing so you
will touch many other lives in a positive way. And
Jodie – your final words on 'AUtism is AUsome' are a
fantastic finale to a fantastic book.

Preface to This Edition

We originally self-published this book in 2021, and we were blown away by the warm reception it received. Many readers, both adults and children, have contacted us to say how much our words helped them to understand their autistic self or the lived experiences of someone they know or support. To say this was unexpected is an understatement, and we have loved hearing about the impact the book has had on so many lives.

We're delighted to have had the opportunity to put together this revised and expanded edition, bringing in new information on monotropism, burnout and school. We've also created a new running order and brought in new design elements — so you're reading the same voices but in an even more user-friendly package! We hope that the information we've provided will continue to help others on their journeys of discovery.

Rose Smitten and Jodie Clarke

Introduction

Rose

My name is Rose and I am eleven years old.

I am autistic and I found this out when I was ten. Like lots of autistic people, I also have attention differences (ADHD).

The reason I'm writing this book is because I want people to understand autism from my perspective. This means that I will be telling you about my autistic self, how it affects me and how I experience the world.

I hope that some of the things I do in life to help me will also help you. I also hope that by hearing about me you will understand yourself or someone you know better.

I have a YouTube channel which is also called 'The Secret Life of Rose'. Please take a look if you would like to know more after reading this book.

JODIE

I am Rose's mum. I am also autistic and have attention differences.

I work as an independent autism specialist, and when Rose was six I realised that what we often saw in her were autistic traits.

Having her formally identified as autistic was somewhat of a struggle: Rose's autism was not visible and was more evident in her 'Ausomeness' than the 'deficits' required for an identification. I am hoping that my experience as a parent and a practitioner will support your journey of discovery, which actually never really ends!

The book is laid out in sections chosen by Rose and me. Each one covers an aspect of Rose's experiences as an autistic child. After Rose's voice comes the 'adult' bit to offer a broader view of the autistic experience.

A Few Words about Words

You may have noticed we use the word 'identification', whereas some may use the word 'diagnosis'. The word 'diagnosis' reminds us of a doctor telling someone they are ill!

We often talk about 'discovering' being autistic rather than being diagnosed with it. We like the word 'discovery' – it makes us think of something exciting, a journey of discovery!

For similar reasons, we talk about being autistic rather than 'having autism'. Again, we don't 'have' an illness, like we have chickenpox or scabies! Autism isn't something that requires treatment – it is a person's identity. This is known as identity-first language, and not only is it preferred by the majority of the autistic community, but for us it also gives a sense of pride and positivity about who we are.

What Is Autism?

Rose

Autism means that your brain works differently than someone who isn't autistic. Although it's also worth saying that even if you meet someone else who is autistic, your brain will still work differently to theirs, too. For example, they may react differently to certain things compared to you: they may hate tight clothes and you may love them.

Much of being autistic is about how we feel things and sense things in the world around us. People talk about this using the words 'sensory differences'.

My brain sees the world in a different way. Sometimes you might feel you belong on a different planet. I sometimes feel like I belong on a planet where people jump about the whole time.

Sometimes an autistic brain can malfunction, meaning the person may have a meltdown, lose their appetite or feel they can't speak. The reason for this is there is so much going on that your brain can't take it all in at once any more. You can sometimes cope for a bit but then your brain gets full and starts to overflow. I use the word overwhelmed to describe this.

There are lots of bright sides to being autistic. You might have a really good memory, you could be really good at a certain subject or skill or be able to really hyperfocus on an subject or activity for a long time. Some autistic people can understand other people's emotions really well and get how they feel.

JODIE

Autism is a different perspective on the world, a different way of sensing what's around you. Very often this sense leads to a mind full of wonder and amazement. Taking in the world in such an intense way means that overload can easily be reached at times. However, this can also result in experiencing incredible levels of joy.

The autistic children I have the pleasure to know offer me the most incredible insight into how their minds work and I'm forever grateful for all they teach me. They are the bravest, most interesting and kindest humans you could meet.

Autism leads to struggles at times, many of which can be adjusted for and avoided if the people around the autistic person are able to reframe and respond with nurture. The golden equation, coined by Dr Luke Beardon, is the thread throughout this book:

Autism + Environment = Outcome

The challenges faced by autistic children come from

the world around them not being conducive to their neurology. In order to enable autistic children to thrive, we have to make changes to their environment. We cannot and should not want to change them as individuals.

With the correct support and love, your child will achieve more than many doctors would have you believe!

There is a saying that goes, 'Sometimes you have to forget what you thought life would be and appreciate what you have got.' On discovering you have an autistic child, this should read, 'You have to forget what you thought life would be, as the journey you will go on will enable growth beyond what you could imagine.'

Having an autistic child and supporting so many families has made me a better parent, a better person and has given me an incredibly deep insight into myself. You can achieve this too. It's also not uncommon for parents to discover their own autistic identity as a result of helping and supporting their autistic children.

Sensory Experiences

Rose

For me, 'sensory' means some things feel really horrible (itchy clothes, like tights) and some things feel really nice (baggy clothes and rollercoasters).

We have eight senses. Five are the ones everyone knows: touch, smell, hearing/sounds, taste and sight. The other ones my mum will tell you the names for!

TOUCH
Anyone touching me at all feels weird – I usually have to 'wipe' it away to take away the feeling.

My legs are really ticklish, even if someone gently touches them. It's not a nice, funny ticklish feeling; it's horrible and makes me upset and uncontrollably kick out. I don't do hugs or kisses, even with my parents, because it feels tingly, which is not nice. I do high fives instead.

Touch also means I find some clothes really uncomfortable. I don't like tight clothes, including tights, jeans, trousers, dresses, skirts, some socks, belts, tight tops. In fact, all I like to wear is comfy, soft, baggy clothes like jogging bottoms, sports leggings, football kits, loose T-shirts and sometimes jumpsuits. I don't like girly clothes and prefer a boyish style.

Touch also impacts my hair. I hate having it cut. I will only wear it in one style, a high ponytail, as otherwise it touches my skin on my neck which makes me itchy.

Getting wet is an odd one – I like swimming pools and hot tubs but I don't like showers or baths. I think it is because most showers or baths are quite small and I don't like small spaces.

The problem with getting wet is that you have to get dry after. The issue with doing this is that the sensation of the towel on my skin feels scratchy so I tend to dry myself by waving the towel around me and sometimes even using the hairdryer.

NOISE

I don't like other people shouting. It hurts my ears, making them feel like they will explode.

I actually like making loud noises myself. I find it funny. It makes me excited but also calms me as it lets all my energy out.

I really **hate** it when people use complicated words or lots of words when they are explaining things to me because I can't understand what they are trying to say. Too many words confuse and overwhelm me and can make me have a meltdown or shutdown.

Noise around me being made by other people or things when I'm trying to concentrate is very annoying because I can't focus on what I'm doing, I can only focus on the noise. This affects me at school and at home, as it can even make watching TV hard.

SMELLS

I don't really have much to say about smells. They don't bother me too much. Although I do really like the smell of lemon and lime.

TASTE/FOOD TEXTURE

I don't like foods all mixed up or touching each other. When we have a roast dinner, I have separate piles for different foods and I eat them separately, for example, all the carrots then all the chicken. I tend to eat the piles in a certain order. I don't eat things like chilli or spaghetti bolognaise where everything is mixed together.

I can really like a food and want to eat it all the time and then I will suddenly go off it. This can annoy my parents, as they buy lots of what I like and then I don't want it any more!

I mostly eat different meals to others in my family. My meals are usually the same each day.

Choosing what to eat is annoying because I never know what I want, even if I look in the fridge and cupboards. This can make me feel really stressed. Having to eat is annoying as it just feels like so much effort. Unless it's sweets and chocolate!!

Foods I don't like make me feel sick, and the thought of eating them is gross. Really gross.

Making me eat foods I don't like is not nice at all. No one should have to eat something that makes them feel sick or that they find gross. I sometimes feel like I need to eat all the time. But sometimes I don't want to eat at all!

VISUAL

I'm good at noticing small details. I'm great at spot the difference games, although I do struggle to find things I have lost, especially amongst mess (e.g., my bedroom!!!).

MOVEMENT (AND PLAY WRESTLING!)

I love moving, jumping, bouncing and clapping my hands. I also love play fighting and going to my dad's homemade gym. Play fighting helps me to make a decision when I am struggling too – this happens a lot. After play fighting I am able to decide.

Chewing things helps me concentrate on schoolwork.

Lifting heavy things in the gym makes me feel more energised and ready for the day. Some mornings I can feel like a slug. When I feel like this, I am very slow-moving; I don't know what to do and can't make any decisions, and this sometimes makes me feel tired. Play fighting or

jumping on the trampoline can help me to feel
less slug-like.

INNER SENSATIONS
Sometimes I don't really know I need the loo
until I'm desperate. I'm not sure I want to tell
people about going to the toilet!!

I don't know if I feel pain differently to
others, as I don't know how others feel pain!
But I do seem to find small cuts very painful
but big scrapes with blood not painful at all!

Sometimes I don't feel pain until I see
the injury!

Sometimes I am hungry **all** the time; sometimes
I forget to eat all day and don't feel hungry
at all!

I don't cope well when it is hot – it feels like
loads of needles stabbing into me.

JODIE

Sensory sensitivities can be one of the biggest causes of anxiety and overwhelm. We cannot underestimate the levels of distress sensory experiences can cause. I would like to emphasise the point that all children should be believed when expressing distress: it's all too easy to discount a sensation that you don't find relatable. Sensory discomfort can be excruciatingly painful.

Sensory-seeking behaviours such as constant movement, fiddling, chewing and making noises are types of stimming. A child is using these to naturally re-regulate or produce joyful feelings.

As parents, it's great to take note of what your child is doing to form the basis of a 'sensory diet'. A sensory diet means you can provide and encourage opportunities for your child to experience these sensations throughout the day and/or to settle them when they are becoming distressed. As with stimming, both sensory avoidance and sensory seeking are forms of communication. Listen to what your child is communicating and respond appropriately.

Sensory profiles change over time, and children can experience heightened sensitivity during times of anxiety. If your child is seemingly more agitated by their clothing than normal or more 'picky' with food, this is likely them communicating that they feel unsettled about something else that is going on for them. Always be curious about what is going on for your child and unpick that with them when they are feeling calm.

The three senses that are less well known are:

- proprioception: the sense that tells us where our body is in space and what it is doing

- vestibular: sensations of body rotation, gravitation, balance and movement that stem from the inner ear

- interoception: our inner sensations that advise us on when our basic needs want attention. These include toileting, eating, drinking, staying warm/not overheating, sleeping and emotional regulation.

Proprioception is an amazing sense. Proprioceptive sensory experiences are fantastic for calming an anxious, unsettled, overwhelmed child, as well as one in a sluggish/shutdown/low-energy state.

Proprioception is a sensory experience that offers high levels of input for the body, such as pushing, pulling, being squashed, trampolining and carrying heavy items. We spend a lot of time play wrestling or doing weights with Rose at various intervals throughout the day. These activities help maintain functional levels of energy and manage her anxiety.

Vestibular seeking children are the ones who love swings and going upside down and can spin for hours with little sensation of being dizzy. Whereas those who are sensitive to the vestibular sense are more likely to suffer motion sickness and be fearful of being too far from the ground, even when being picked up by an adult.

Interoception is a really important sense to be aware of. Simply put, it is our inner sensations that indicate to us what basic needs need to be met. These include hunger, thirst, needing the toilet, needing to sleep and indicating pain. Sensory differences mean that autistic people can be both hypersensitive to these signals, for example, feeling starving at the first twinge of hunger, and hyposensitive, for example, not realising you need the loo until you are desperate and then struggling to get there in time! Interoception differences also impact emotions, which we cover later in their own section.

Stimming

Rose

Stimming is an action or a noise that you repeat over and over again when you are excited, worried or angry.

This could be jumping up and down, making lots of random noises, clapping your hands, flapping your arms, chewing things, kicking your legs, biting your nails, biting your lip, fiddling with your hair, repeating phrases from the TV, saying the same word over and over again, rocking backwards and forwards, bouncing, picking, watching the same bit of a TV show over and over again, opening of your mouth into unusual poses, standing on your head, talking in accents or a baby voice and many, many more.

Stimming helps me to let out energy, to focus and concentrate, and to feel more calm and chilled.

You shouldn't worry about stimming; you should just do it! (Although you may want to explain to your friends what it's all about!)

Stimming makes me feel zoned out of the world and I can only think of the thing I am happy about – it blocks anything else out.

If I'm stimming because I'm not feeling good, like if I'm nervous, then flapping my hands or fiddling with something distracts me from the bad feelings and blocks them out.

JODIE

Stimming (self-stimulatory behaviours) is a way of regulating emotions, good or bad.

Stimming should never be disallowed or disciplined. If it causes harm to someone, such as skin picking/self-harm, then a replacement stim offering similar sensory feedback should be explored. Stimming should never be discouraged due to fear of judgement from others; instead, onlookers should have stimming explained to them.

Stimming is an expression or communication of emotion, and emotions should always be embraced.

It's helpful to take note of stims and when they occur. Determining if a stim indicates distress or excitement means you can act accordingly. For example, if your child is communicating distress, then you can support them by removing them from the source of distress. If a child is expressing enjoyment, then you make a mental note of what your child is experiencing and give more opportunity to engage in this.

Stimming behaviours are closely linked with sensory profiles of autistic people; therefore, it can be helpful for both parents and children to be aware of their own stims and to use them as coping tools in managing emotions.

As well as providing emotional regulation, stimming can support information processing, so encouraging stimming to aid listening, focus and carrying out tasks is also really important.

Emotions

Rose

I am either really happy or really angry, sad or worried. I can tell them apart but only when they are really strong. This means I don't always know what I feel and what I'm upset about.

I don't feel my emotions slowly coming; I just suddenly feel them really strongly. This makes it difficult to calm myself down before I get really cross. It's hard to use any sensory toys to calm myself down because by the time I need them I am too angry to remember I need them and to get them.

Meditation doesn't help me **at all** because it bores me. Instead, I need movement to help me calm. I enjoy bouncing on the trampoline and jumping around the house.

I only know how I feel if the feeling is very

strong. This means that often I don't know how
I feel. My mum will ask me but I will just say
I don't know. If others ask me, I just say I'm
fine, because it's easier than explaining that I
don't know how I feel.

JODIE

Recognising emotions is linked to sensory experiences. Interoception is the body's internal signals and sensations that tell us how we are feeling – whether that's how hungry we feel, how cold we feel or how happy we feel. Interoception differences in autism play a vital role in children becoming emotionally dysregulated.

When talking with families about emotions, many report having a child who goes from zero to a hundred in a split second. I frequently ask about whether a child's responses to hunger or needing the toilet follow a similar pattern to the ramping up of emotions.

For example, your child may not think they need a wee, and then two seconds later they are bursting or having accidents. Maybe they also struggle to remember to eat or will go from being fine to being so ravenous and 'hangry'. These could indicate that your child is hyposensitive to their internal signals (interoception).

Equally, a child can be hypersensitive, and so the first pang of hunger can lead to them feeling like they need to eat all the time. Remember that a child's hypo- and hypersensitivities can change from one day to the next! Us parents are very often on the back foot.

Now, if we consider this in relation to emotions, some children have no sensation of happy or angry until they are hyperactively bouncing round the room or exploding into an almighty rage. Imagine how scary this must be as a child when one second you feel fine and the next you feel completely overwhelmed and consumed by an anger that is completely outside your control.

There is also the consideration of alexithymia, which is the inability to recognise, understand and communicate your emotions (or any one of these). This is not unique to autism but is often a co-occurring condition and worth reading up on. The interplay between alexithymia and the interoceptive sense can make emotions feel scary and overwhelming. Awareness of this is vital for supporting your child with their emotions.

Empathy

Rose

Empathy is knowing how other people feel.

I am good at this. I can notice small changes in how people look and have learnt what this means and how they might feel. When people are sad, they act differently to how they normally act.

If it's someone I don't know, then I don't know how they feel by looking at them, as I don't know what they look like normally, unless it's really obvious how they are feeling, like if they are really crying.

Sometimes other people's feelings confuse me. This happens a lot when I am watching the TV. All the crying during Britain's Got Talent is annoying because I don't understand why someone would cry at a song.

JODIE

Many autistic children are hypersensitive to the emotions of others. It can be almost like a super sense. This is known as hyperempathy, and it enables many autistic people to actually feel the emotions of others.

This can be emotionally draining and exhausting. This in turn can lead to children shutting or melting down in response to the emotions of others, particularly if they are unable to offload these emotions through communication. This can lead to the misconception that autistic people have no empathy, as their responses seem inappropriate.

Rose has learnt emotions through studying patterns of behaviour and noticing changes in patterns to people's behaviours. When people don't follow these patterns, mismatches of understanding can occur.

We witness her confusion during TV shows as she becomes agitated. Rose dislikes and will avoid watching films because of this. Alexithymia, as discussed in our 'Emotions' section, is worth reading up on if this is relatable.

Executive Functioning/ Organisation

Rose

Organising myself is hard, because I forget stuff a lot. I forget my homework, my football kit, my lunchbox, my school bag – I basically leave things behind wherever I go! I even went swimming once and forgot my swim bag, but then I realised after twenty minutes of standing in the changing rooms that I hadn't forgotten it but had just left it in the car. I had forgotten that I hadn't forgotten it!!!! Ha ha.

Even when my mum reminds me, I can forget what she has said seconds after – this is because I sometimes don't even process what she has said. I don't do this on purpose; it's just that I'm thinking about other things all the time.

Tidying up my bedroom is absolutely impossible sometimes because starting jobs when there is lots to do is **really** hard. It helps me if someone starts the job with me and gives me smaller parts of it to do at a time.

When my bedroom is tidy, everything is put away and I can't find anything. If I had my way, tidying wouldn't even be a word.

Another part of this is that my idea of time can be a bit off in that I often leave things until the last minute, not realising how long it may take me to do them.

I am very easily distracted. Hang on, just trying to watch something on the telly! I struggle to concentrate, which means I often start something but don't finish it. Anything can distract me, like something around me that catches my eye.

When I went to a mainstream school, the older kids had break earlier than us and if I saw them on the field playing football I would get distracted from my schoolwork and watch them. In my English room, there were poems on the wall, and I was easily distracted by them and would sit and read them when I should've been listening.

Sometimes I can just be staring into space, distracted by the thoughts that are in my head... Sorry, just need to speak to my dog! Then I realise someone has told me to do something. Oddly, sometimes I still know what they have told me to do even though I haven't been listening!

JODIE

A person with executive functioning difficulties can sometimes be deemed lazy or disorganised. Sadly, many are made to feel this way, as those around them don't realise this is actually due to executive functioning challenges and is not a choice.

Executive functioning can be impacted by anxiety, stress, autism and ADHD, so if you have a child with one or a combination of these the impact on them day-to-day can be significant.

Executive functioning can impact (amongst other things): working memory, time management, task initiation, staying on task, emotional regulation, switching tasks and transitions.

Putting all your energy into one activity can make it hard to then move suddenly to something else. This is linked to monotropism: a theory of autism that suggests it involves tunnel-like attention and is worth parents reading up on.

If you recognise that your child struggles with any or all of these, supporting them by breaking tasks down into small chunks, sharing tasks to reduce the mental load, using visuals such as picture timelines or checklists and setting alarms/external reminders can really help and may also offer them some independence.

Predictable, known routines can also support executive functioning, as they become more automatic and use less mental load once they are established.

Monotropism

Rose

My brain has had various different focuses since I was young... one of my first ones was snails. This was from when I was a toddler until primary school. I kept them as pets and would keep them in my room. I would even have them sitting with me at the dinner table while I ate! I had a very small one called 'Tiny'... one day I lost him! I was really upset. Me and my mum had to look all over the house for him... we eventually found him attached to my baby brother's bouncy seat in the front room!

Since then, I have had a few other big interests including chickens, football (Arsenal in particular), playing guitar, Marvel and editing on my PC. Currently I have the two interests, Marvel and editing, but all of my other interests tended to be one at a time. I would really focus on them and learn all about them. My parents would buy me everything I needed

linked to them (football kits, music equipment!)
and soon enough I would be done with that
interest and move on to something new!

JODIE

Monotropism is the most encompassing theory of autism and has been developed by an autistic person called Dinah Murray.

Monotropic neurology is described as having a tunnel-vision mind. Autistic brains are able to put all their focus into one thing. Our brains have numerous attention tunnels. Autistic brains are able to take all their mental attention down one tunnel. On the positive side, this enables us to hyperfocus on things that bring us joy. Being in these 'joy tunnels' of attention is a fantastic feeling and can sometimes allow us to block out the world around us and become fixated on the activity that has drawn us in. (I use the word 'us' as these issues are faced by all autistic people, children and adults.)

Monotropic learning and thinking styles, when allowed to flow, can lead to great successes in our chosen areas for some; often these achievements and skills become self-taught. This may be relatable to parents when considering how expert their child becomes on certain topics or games, for example.

If we allow the natural monotropic flow of our children's brains in their learning, we will likely see them thrive more readily than if we expect them to focus on a wide array of topics with little depth (which is how learning is laid out in the national curriculum). Child-led, interest-led learning is the ideal for our autistic children.

On the flip side, this hyperfocus can sometimes lead to distressing experiences caused by our environment. It's hard if not impossible for us to simply 'ignore' the noise, feel, smell, etc. of something that has drawn all our attention.

During periods of hyperfocus, we can sometimes switch off from our bodily needs and functions, such as using the toilet or feeding ourselves – essentially, meeting our basic needs. This doesn't mean we need to be dragging our children out of hyperfocus. Instead, we should be mindful that when we call them for dinner, pulling away their attention from something in which they have found monotropic joy can be really distressing. It requires time, patience and acceptance.

Masking

Rose

Masking is when you're upset or angry or worried and you act like you are happy. It can also mean that you act and behave like other children in your surroundings, but I don't tend to do this as much, because my friends seem to accept who I am even though I am different from them. Although I don't often stim in front of them.

When I mask, at the end of the day it makes me feel worn out because you're acting an emotion that you are not actually feeling. To do it I just pretend like nothing has happened to upset me and I just smile and carry on as normal. I keep the feelings of upset inside.

I go to an online school now, but when I was at a mainstream school I had a card to help me share my feelings: one side was red and the other was green. When I was upset or worried or angry, I turned it to show the red side. Then I got to go outside onto the playground and kick around my football for five minutes. This made me feel calmer because I was focusing on the ball and not on how I was feeling. It also gave me a break from the classroom, which helped.

When I was younger, I was scared to use the card because I thought people might ask me questions about it and wonder what it is. I was also worried that teachers might ask me what was wrong, and I can't tell people about how I'm feeling. Teachers and children in my online school now know I am autistic and that has been a good thing for me.

JODIE

Masking is incredibly common within the autistic community. Masking is a suppression of self: emotions, interests, needs and identity. Masking is often subconscious and is a strategy that develops to protect the individual from harm, ridicule, discipline, uncomfortable attention, questions or comments and bullying. Essentially, it is a survival strategy to manage the non-autistic world.

Masking causes exhaustion, a loss of self-identity and anxiety. In the long term, it can cause autistic burnout and mental health struggles.

It's vital that parents and professionals are aware of masking. If you are a parent whose child is well behaved in school and lets it all out on you at home, it can be hard to access assessments and support.

Children should be supported to unmask in the safety of those who know and love them. When others become accepting of their differences, autistic children feel more able to unmask at school and with friends.

Unfortunately, unmasking is hard when it can be so instinctive and unconscious.

School

Rose

I found school really stressful, as there were lots of children and it was really loud and busy. The work was really hard, as I didn't get any help in class and some teachers were not understanding of me and didn't get the stress I was under.

This resulted in me being worried and scared every day and not feeling able to go to school. I was made to feel like I wasn't very clever, but I now know it's actually the way I was taught was not right for me to be able to learn. Basically, there was nothing wrong with me but rather the problem was with how things were being taught to me, as well as the actual school building itself.

You want to feel happy so you can learn without getting overwhelmed by the work, teachers, friends or place.

Assemblies were one of the most overwhelming things for me, as you are being made to sit on the floor cross-legged very close to other children and in a loud hall. Sitting cross-legged is fine for me but a lot of children find it uncomfortable, which makes it even more stressful.

In primary school we were made to sing. I didn't like this at all since I don't like singing, especially when I am around loads of other people. I also remember children being told off if they weren't singing, which just made things worse - knowing if I didn't sing I would be told off.

Some teachers are really annoying because they don't understand that some children need teaching differently. Teachers who were shouty would make me feel sad because the noise would hurt my ears and I was scared they would shout at me. Many teachers would make me feel sad, but the trouble is when I was at school, I wouldn't show it because I was too scared to. I would mask.

I have had a good teacher. They didn't shout, they made things interesting and were funny. When I was in their class, I felt like they got me and understood me. Although it was still hard, as they had to teach certain things in certain ways, it felt like they tried their best to make it work for me.

I now don't attend a typical school. I learn online and have tutors/teachers who are also autistic, which is great as they get me and teach me in a way that works for my brain. This has made all the difference to me.

The teachers have also been able to let me use my interest in my learning, like when I was really into football, in maths, we looked at all the Arsenal players' wages and compared the wages of the men's team versus the women's team! I feel much more confident and happy doing things this way. I have also tried out different types of schools, such as farm schools and forest schools, which I have enjoyed.

JODIE

Schools can be incredibly stressful and exhausting places for neurodivergent people. The social, sensory and executive functioning demands all compounding each other can lead to overwhelm, anxiety, masking, stress and exhaustion. This was very much the case for Rose, and although Rose wanted to go to school to see her friends, the demand and lack of understanding meant it was not safe for her emotionally.

There are so many restraints within our education system that mean even the most incredible teachers are up against it when it comes to fully supporting our autistic children and teaching them in a way that is conducive to their neurology. Large class sizes and the pace and rigidity of the national curriculum are just a couple of examples. But unfortunately, educators are not educated in autistic experience, and those who have been trained most likely will have been trained in outdated and harmful theories and approaches.

School trauma is common in the autistic community,

and sadly, while many schools still take very behaviourist approaches, this will continue.

Rose has accessed alternative provision for some time now, which has given her the opportunity to thrive. This wasn't easy to achieve (as any parent who has been within the special educational needs and disabilities (SEND) system will know), but like so, so many parents across the country, I had little choice due to the detrimental impact on her mental health.

I have so much I could say here on the challenges our children face in our current mainstream education system, but that would be a book in itself. However, my website is full of information, talks and writing on this: www.jodiesmitten.co.uk.

Friends, Friendships and Socialising

Rose

I don't like making new friends – it's difficult, I'm not sure why. I just find it hard to speak to people I don't know.

I like to be friends with people who have similar likes to me, as then we have something to talk about. If someone doesn't have the same interests as me, I don't think I'd have anything to say to them. If someone was into girly stuff, they may just want to talk about make-up and doing hair, and I'm not really interested in that, so I wouldn't know what to say.

When I have a friend round, I like to have a plan of what we are going to do, because otherwise we may get a bit bored, and I don't like being bored. This would make me worry that my friend is bored and doesn't want to be around me. My plan is usually written out with different sections and things to do, with a timetable at the bottom.

Talking to people I don't know is absolutely the most frightening thing in the whole entire world. If someone speaks to me that I don't know I have to talk back and it feels scary. If my mum is with me, it feels a bit better, as my mum will sometimes speak for me.

Some people are scarier to speak to than others, like all the teachers at school, except for teachers who have taught me and know me. I often go really quiet and can't get my words out – this is weird, as I can actually become unable to talk and my brain can't think.

JODIE

Rose has been mute in some situations since she was a toddler, often acting as though no-one has even said anything to her and redirecting her attention elsewhere. When her sister was born, Rose would often ignore any interaction with an unfamiliar person and simply put her head into the pram and talk to her sister.

Mutism commonly occurs with autism. To ease anxiety, a child should never be coaxed into talking or reprimanding for not being able to, as mutism is not a choice. In the case of buying something, Rose is able to manage independently as she knows this interaction will follow a particular protocol.

Social aspects of independence can be practised at home during role-play. If Rose is embarking on something new independently, we talk through the language that will help in the situation. This is important for personal safety. It is important to work out with a child where they would go or what they would say if they needed help when out and about without a familiar adult.

Periods of socialising can lead to exhaustion and a need for recharging in the form of alone time/time on electronics or engaging in their special interests. All of these activities allow the child control and predictability, which are much needed after a period of time in unpredictable and exhausting settings.

It's really important that autistic children are given the opportunity to spend time with other autistic children, ideally those who share the same interest.

Assuming that an autistic child will get along with any other autistic child is erroneous, but it is important to consider the double empathy problem, introduced by an autistic academic named Damian Milton. The focus of the double empathy problem is that autistic people have social differences, not social 'deficits'. When autistic people socialise with other autistic people, social differences are not apparent because they share the same social skill set. There is a mutual understanding and acceptance that an autistic person may not encounter when around non-autistics.

Often autistic children naturally gravitate towards each other. Many children I work with have autistic best friends without either of them being actually aware of the other's autistic identity. This has all sorts of amazing benefits: they 'get' each other, they feel connected to another individual and they accept each other's quirks, all of which are so good for positive self-identity and mental health.

Burnout

Rose

So, this was how autistic burnout was for me: I wasn't able to leave the house much, or to do much at all really. I didn't have the energy to get dressed or washed. I found it hard to eat and decide what to eat, I was eating even less foods than normal. I was too scared to sleep in my own room and slept on my parents' floor. I would be up really late, finding it harder than normal to fall asleep (although it always takes me a couple of hours to drop off to sleep). I didn't see any friends.

During this time, I was a lot more anxious about everything! I spent this time feeling constantly sad and worried. I wasn't able to go to school.

My parents let me sit in bed all day. For a time, the only food I wanted was McDonald's so me and my mum would go to the drive through quite a lot. I spent **a lot** of time on my phone

playing Roblox and a lot of time on my own.
I spent a lot of time seeming like I was doing
nothing **but** this all helped me a lot.

JODIE

Thinking back on this time is hard. Rose's burnout
was heartbreaking. As parents, we send our children
to school because we think that in doing so we are
enabling them to have a positive future. Sadly, for
many of us the opposite is truer. Feelings of guilt
flooded me. No parent should have to see their child in
such distress.

Burnout affects so many autistic children and yet it
is so often missed or misunderstood. This can lead
to harmful approaches and attitudes. Research into
autistic burnout in adults is limited but research in
children is almost non-existent. Yet autistic burnout is
very real.

Signs your child may be in or heading towards autistic
burnout:

- Unable to manage school

- An increase in frequency or severity of meltdowns/
  shutdowns

- Significantly heightened sensory sensitivities

- Low mood

- Feelings of/acting on feelings of harming themselves

- Decreased ability to carry out self-care tasks

- Changes or restrictions to eating

- Changes or increased sleep difficulties

- Social exhaustion/decreased tolerance or motivation to be around others.

Burnout recovery involves a child resting at home and having a complete reduction in all demands, autonomy over what they can and cannot manage, recharge time with special interests and complete acceptance of the mental health crisis they are in from those around them.

Although autistic burnout is not (currently) a diagnosable or often recognised mental health condition, there are many blogs, talks and writings on the subject by autistic people, which are most definitely worthwhile googling to gain further insight.

Meltdowns

Rose

A meltdown is when I get overwhelmed and start to feel angry. I start shouting, crying and throwing things sometimes. My head feels like it has been overtaken by angriness. I can't control it – it just happens and seems to come out of nowhere.

The things that trigger them are: too many people being around me and talking to me, not understanding what someone is trying to say to me or a bad day at school. If I have been masking, when I get home my emotions can all burst out as a meltdown.

It helps me if I am left alone and people don't talk to me. If people ask me if I'm okay I get more cross, because it's pretty obvious that I'm not okay. People asking me, 'What's wrong?' can make me feel worse because sometimes I don't even know what's wrong. Saying nothing to me until I start to feel calmer is better. When I'm calmer, someone saying, 'How can I help you?' is good.

Other things that help me are going to a small space and cuddling my favourite soft toy. The screaming and shouting can help me to get it all out. I often feel tired after but also better for letting it all out.

JODIE

Each child differs in terms of the best way to support them during a meltdown. Rose has covered the most important point – that a meltdown is a neurological response to a perceived fear and is therefore not within a child's control.

Essentially, a meltdown is like a panic attack. Therefore, we must respond accordingly and not punish, shout or escalate. This is particularly difficult when a child is putting themselves or others at risk of harm. As a parent, our fear response can then also be triggered, making us unable to regulate ourselves in order to support and nurture our child. It is the job of us as the parents to practise calmness in our response to meltdowns; this takes some practice.

Everyone's safety is essential during this time, and moving items and other children to another space is often better than trying to remove a child in meltdown, as physical contact without consent can be further triggering.

Some children need a trusted adult to be nearby; some prefer to be alone. Some prefer a deep pressure hug or weighted blanket; others prefer no touch whatsoever.

We have learnt what works for Rose through conversation during calm times. Many parents have reported to me that their child will follow them when they try to move away from their child in meltdown; this is because you are their safe person. For some children, leaving them alone can create further fear and send a message that you don't want to be around them unless they are fine and happy. Again, this is only the case for some, and some children actually want to be left alone.

The Dos of supporting a meltdown differ between individuals. The Do Nots, however, apply more generally: don't ask questions such as, 'What's wrong? Are you okay?' Don't punish. Don't shout.

Simply nurture in the way you would care for a distressed newborn baby.

Negative responses to meltdowns that are outside of children's control can lead to negative cycles.

Remember, children know right from wrong, and a child will do right when they can.

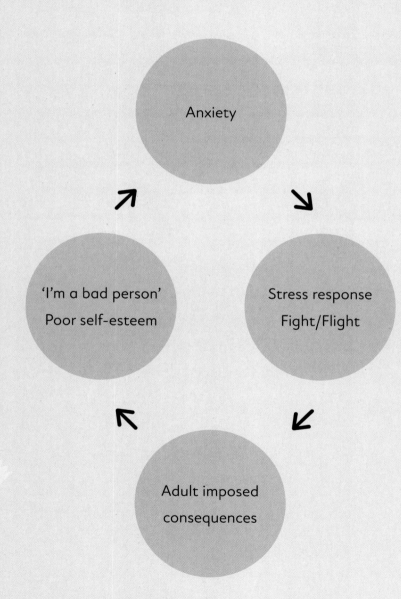

Anxiety

'I'm a bad person'
Poor self-esteem

Stress response
Fight/Flight

Adult imposed
consequences

Shutdowns

Rose

This is where you become so overwhelmed that you become like a robot, you hide, you don't talk to anyone even if they talk to you, you don't want anything – you just want to be alone and for people to leave you alone. I am usually still and may be curled up in a ball. I may sometimes make funny noises such as repetitive groaning if I'm in a safe place.

Things that help me in a shutdown are pretty much the same as when I'm in meltdown. I feel tired afterwards.

JODIE

A shutdown can be considered an internalised meltdown. On the outside, you may look calm and 'fine' or you may look absent or spaced out. Internally, you may feel suppressed anger or rage even (although this is more likely masking than a full shutdown). Or a numbness that comes from the brain going into self-preservation mode, taking over to protect you. During shutdowns, a child may be unable to speak or move and, like during meltdowns, they will be unable to process or listen.

Although shutdowns may not be experienced as concerning from the outsider's perspective, they are as harmful as meltdowns. In fact, one could argue they are more harmful, as they can often go completely unnoticed by the onlooker, meaning no emotional or regulation support is offered. As you can imagine, there are links between shutdowns and masking. If adults recognise the signs of a shutdown, a child should be safely supported as they would be in meltdown.

AUtism is AUsome!

Rose

Being autistic means I can do things others can't, like I can remember things from a really long time ago, in detail. I remember the first day back at school in 2015 – we were walking to school, and I felt excited because I would get to write 2015 in my schoolbook instead of 2014. Another time I remember walking to school, and it was quite frosty and cold, and we were talking about whether robins come out in the winter – bit random! I often remember conversations.

My great hearing means I'm like a dog, I can hear things that are far away. The best bit about this is I can hear exactly what my mum and dad are saying to each other in the evenings when I'm in bed, even though my bedroom is in the loft!

Being autistic means I'm different from

everyone else. This is great, as if you are the same as everyone else it's boring! Knowing you are autistic is even better, as then you don't have to try and be like everyone else – you can just be your own cool, different self.

Before I found out I am autistic I felt weird, in a bad way – I thought I had to be like everybody else, and this didn't feel very nice. Now I know I'm autistic I don't have to pretend that I'm the same as everyone else. I'm happier now.

JODIE

Rose and the children I work with are **incredible**.
They are creative, resilient and brave. Every day
these little people face a chaotic, unpredictable and
uncompromising world! These children constantly have
to adapt and adjust their natural ways to suit others.

Their worlds can very quickly and easily become
overwhelming and unbearable. The non-autistics
around them don't have the same experiences, so
they expect the autistic child to just 'get on with it'
or 'get over it', and then deem them 'challenging' if
they have a meltdown or refuse to engage. Very often
these children aren't empathised with – which is ironic,
considering the myth around autistic people not
having empathy!

I refer you back to the golden equation coined by
Dr Luke Beardon:

Autism + Environment = Outcome

For an autistic child to thrive, learn, enjoy life and

be free of mental health illnesses, it is vital that their world (environment) meets their needs, adjusts to their differences and not only understands but also accepts who they are.

This is the responsibility of all the adults in their life, not the child. We must adjust, we must accept, we must advocate.

Final Thoughts

Keep being AUsome!

Rose

Never let your parenting be swayed by other people's judgements of it. Nobody knows your child like you do!

Jodie